Ideas & Action
GEORGE P. SHULTZ

Ideas & Action, George P. Shultz
was produced by Free To Choose Press,
Erie, Pennsylvania.

Bob Chitester, *President*; James Tusty, *Project Leader*;
Anna deVries, *Editor*; Oberlander Group, *Design Firm*;
John Oberlander, *President*; Lynne Allard, *Designer*;
Chad Bradt, *Production Designer*;
Wordsmithing, *Research, Editing, Wordsmithing*;
Grace Hawes, *Archivist*;
Russell Rader, *Archivist Photographer*.

First Printing

Published in the United States by Free To Choose Press, an
educational initiative of Free To Choose Network. Free To
Choose Network is a not-for-profit 501(c)3 U.S. corporation.

ISBN 978-0-578-05795-8

Free To Choose Press
2002 Filmore Avenue
Suite 1
Erie, PA 16506

www.freetochoose.net

OUR PURPOSE / To use accessible and entertaining media
to build popular support for personal, economic and political freedom. We believe these freedoms are interdependent
and must be sustained by the rule of law.

Ideas & Action
GEORGE P. SHULTZ
featuring the
10 Commandments of Negotiations

Free To
CHOOSE
P R E S S

Table of Contents

FOREWORD /
Henry A. Kissinger
Former Secretary of State

The transition from the life of the university to that of politics seems natural but is, in fact, very complex. The academic can choose his subject; the policymaker has it imposed on him. The academic can allocate the time he needs to his project. The policymaker is always under the deadline of evolving events. The academic is in a position to alter his perceptions. The policymaker is constrained by the commitment of others; his turning radius is like that of a great ocean liner. The academic is in a position to concentrate on a great vision; the policymaker needs to hedge as well against the consequences of failure. There are some experiments he cannot try because the penalty for being wrong is too severe.

No one has connected academic to public life more successfully or more seamlessly than George Shultz. He held four cabinet posts; he has been the confidant of presidents of both our political parties. His great contribution to government has been to leaven the inevitable tactics of the day with the perspectives of wisdom and balance. Since leaving full-time government service, he has had no peer in relating the conceptual to the political. On a series of issues at the cutting edge of our national challenges, George Shultz has provided leadership and vision. Demography, the national economy, and, in recent years, how to rid the world of the scourge of nuclear warfare have benefited from his unique style of leadership, based on a rare ability to evoke from others the best of which they are capable.

Effective leadership must operate on many levels. Above all, there is the requirement for vision. "Where are we trying to go?" is the seminal question. Without an answer to it, efforts are random; the national debate, if it takes place at all, emphasizes the peripheral, and negotiations concentrate on technique. As chairman of groups devoting themselves to policy studies, George Shultz's extraordinary ability to ask the penetrating question keeps discussions focused, and his patience encourages intellectual enterprises. On the nuclear issue, his goodwill and dedication transformed what started as an academic exploration of the lessons of the Reykjavik conference between Ronald Reagan and Mikhail Gorbachev into an action program for dealing with the spread of nuclear weapons, which has become the basis of global efforts.

George Shultz has been able to translate vision into operational programs because, due to his broad experience, he can rally significant constituencies within the bureaucratic structure, the legislative process, and, finally, public opinion.

The principles of negotiation put forward by George Shultz in this work demonstrate these qualities. He emphasizes that negotiation is about persuasion, not technique; that it reflects ultimately moral components like reliability, steadfastness, and credibility; and that it must relate power to morality.

It shows, above all, why George Shultz has had such a remarkable impact over so many decades. The ultimate task of a leader is to take his society from where it is to where it has never been. At first, this journey is lonely because most people cling to the familiar. Those who move society inspire the courage to explore and the tenacity to persist. In the decades I have had the good fortune to work side by side with George Shultz, I have learned a great deal from the maxims he puts forward in this volume.

Foreword /
Dianne Feinstein
U.S. Senator

George Shultz is one of the most influential leaders of our time. There is no living person I know of who has held more senior administration posts or who has garnered more respect from both sides of the political spectrum. He has worn a number of different hats: soldier, scholar, corporate executive, cabinet secretary, and elder statesman. Through it all, he has managed to be simultaneously a man of big ideas and of concrete results.

In this latest book, George shares some of his formative experiences at the negotiating table and lays out a road map of how to solve difficult problems. He offers up a new "Ten Commandments of Success in Negotiations" for leaders and decision makers in all walks of life. In example after example, he articulates the value of embracing bold vision and confident leadership tempered by patience and achievable objectives. This book makes for an absorbing and educational read.

Possessing a shrewd perspective developed over a long career in public service, including four cabinet-level positions, he takes the reader behind the scenes of some of the most complex and fascinating policy challenges of our time—from the desegregation of Southern schools and the air-traffic controller strike to the Reykjavik Summit and Camp David. This is a book that is at once distinctly pragmatic and deeply personal. One quickly comes to appreciate the author's keen insights, poignant recollections, and extraordinary determination.

Of particular interest to me is his long involvement in the nuclear nonproliferation debate.

Hardly alone in being profoundly affected by the bombings of Hiroshima and Nagasaki, he is one who has worked to ensure that such terrible events never again happen. First, at the side of President Reagan, and through every administration since, this former secretary of state has played a pivotal role in efforts to make the world safer from nuclear weapons.

The Cold War is over, but the national security threat remains. Together, the United States and Russia possess roughly 95 percent of the world's nuclear weapons, and there are serious political and procedural hurdles that must be overcome before we can wind down these deadly arsenals.

We no longer fear the threat of an all-out nuclear war, but the likelihood that the United States will be attacked by terrorists with a nuclear, chemical, or biological weapon has increased. We must do all that we can to keep the world's most dangerous weapons out of the world's most dangerous hands.

Today, George, as one of the so-called "Four Horsemen"—together with William J. Perry, Sam Nunn, and Henry Kissinger—continues to persuade policymakers of the dangers of proliferation and the need to take decisive action.

As one who believes passionately in the vision of a nuclear-free world, I am grateful for his continued dedication to stopping the spread of these destructive weapons.

This book is a must-read for everyone in public service today and for anyone interested in a career in public service tomorrow.

FOREWORD /
William J. Perry
Former Secretary of Defense

This book is an extraordinary account of the negotiating techniques practiced by one of America's most successful diplomats. But it is more than that. As you read this book, you will discover that George Shultz is first of all a patriot, in the best sense of that word. He deeply loves his country and has demonstrated that through a life of exceptional service to it. In World War II, he served as a Marine and participated in some of the bloody landings on Pacific islands. After he finished his military service and university education, he served in distinguished positions in industry and academia. But he never failed to answer his government's calls, serving two presidents in cabinet-level positions and other presidents in key advisory roles.

George Shultz, while serving his country, also serves his party. But he never lets his party loyalty conflict with his country's interests. He has teamed up with another Republican and two Democrats in working to reduce nuclear dangers, but he is always clear that he does not regard this team as "bipartisan," but rather "nonpartisan." That is, some problems are so important that they transcend party loyalties.

George has been a remarkably successful diplomat, and this book gives some fascinating examples of how his negotiations served his diplomacy. It becomes clear from these examples that when he negotiates he starts off by being a good listener. And as he listens, he puts himself in the shoes of the other speaker, and of the other country. So when he is ready to speak, he offers proposals that reflect the interests of the other speaker's country, as well as the interests of his own country.

There are other qualities of George Shultz that are not explicit, but are clearly implicit in the examples in this book. Most importantly, he is a brilliant leader. He can rise above the details of a complex problem to see its essential features. He can envision broad solutions to problems and articulate his vision in ways that inspire others on his negotiating team to support him. When his team has a failure, he accepts the responsibility; when it succeeds, he gives the credit to his team. Not only negotiators, but government leaders of all ages and all ranks, can profit from his examples.

Fri. June 25

Today was the day—I told Al H. I had decided to accept his resignation. He didn't seem surprised but he said his differences were on policy and then said we didn't agree on China or Russia etc. I made a simple announcement to the press and said I was nominating Geo. ~~[illegible]~~ Shultz for the job. I'd called him & like the patriot he is he said "yes".

This has been a heavy load. Up to Camp David where we were in time to see Al read his letter of resignation on T.V. Jim told it was his 4th re-write. Apparently his 1st was pretty strong—then he thought better of it. I must say it was O.K. He gave only one reason & did say there was a disagreement on foreign policy. Actually the only disagreement was over whether I made policy or the Sec. of State did.

Ronald Reagan's Personal Diary

June 25, 1982

George Shultz being sworn in as Secretary of State, July 16, 1982.

As President of Bechtel.

As Secretary of State on Air Force One.

As Dean of the Graduate School of Business, the University of Chicago.

INTRODUCTION /

We have grown accustomed to drawing a bright divide between the world of ideas, a world dominated by ivory towers, and the world of action, a world dominated by oval offices, market floors, and fields of battle. My life and career, however, have known no such bright dividing line. The university world, the world of ideas, was the base from which I went into four different cabinet positions and the presidency of a large global corporation. Upon leaving the post of secretary of state in 1989, I returned to the university where my life continues to be diverse—a little government, a little business, and lots of university.

My education included study at MIT for a doctorate in economics, which included mediation and arbitration. I was exposed to lots of negotiations, to the problems created by plant closures, and I took part in the creation of manpower training programs. Earlier, I had fought in the Pacific as a U.S. Marine after graduating from Princeton, where the motto "Princeton in the Nation's Service" influenced my thinking and my aspirations. I have benefited enormously from having had the chance to move back and forth from a life of ideas to a life of action, from a world of reflection to a world of high-level decision making.

All of these experiences had a major impact on my way of approaching problems and on my style of work in large governmental, university, and business organizations. These jobs gave me a chance to put ideas into action and, in the process, to test and refine the ideas and to develop new ones. Major themes in my work and life are the interplay of ideas and action and the effort to learn as much as possible from every experience. Some of my most memorable learning experiences are captured in the stories that follow.

SECTION 1 /

Keys to Good Management

PARTICIPATION / My labor and industrial relations days taught me about the magic of participation. A case in point were the Hawthorne Experiments, designed to study the impact of changes in lighting on productivity. Results of the study, a surprise to the researchers, showed the powerful effect of recognizing workers and listening to their suggestions. I also learned from Joe Scanlon, who joined us at MIT from his role as research director of the United Steelworkers Union. He had a remarkable ability to change the atmosphere in the workplace by conveying to workers, *You matter. You have a stake.* I worked with Joe as he developed his Scanlon Plan, which included workers in making decisions about how their jobs were structured. The results were dramatic.

I reflected on these ideas as I assumed various managerial positions. I was convinced that if I could create a work situation where everybody, including me, was learning something, I would always have a hot group. People love to learn, to be involved, and to be recognized. As a manager, you find that if you pay a little attention to your employees, you just might learn something. So the Scanlon Plan and the Hawthorne Experiments had a major, beneficial impact on my managerial style.

YOU MATTER. YOU HAVE A STAKE.

Ronald Reagan shared this view. Visitors to the Oval Office were greeted by a sign, placed prominently on his desk, which read, "There is no limit to what a man can do or where he can go if he doesn't mind who gets the credit."

RESPONSIBILITY / In the labor relations field, the importance of union and management leaders making their own decisions, and then taking responsibility for their agreements, is well recognized. You do a better job administering an agreement that is yours—the ownership principle at work. Sometimes, however, it takes a conflict to sober up people. So be it. Mediation and arbitration are available, but responsibility needs to be accompanied by a willingness to strike or take a strike. If you won't fight for what you believe in, you won't get very far. If the government makes a practice of intervening to prevent strikes or business failures, that sense of responsibility is dulled and the system changes in undesirable ways.

As a professor at the University of Chicago, I was particularly critical of extensive interventions by the Kennedy and Johnson administrations into big-time labor disputes made on the grounds that a strike would be disruptive to the economy. Of course, that meant that government would be involved in the terms of the ultimate outcome. Furthermore, intervention would lead inevitably to erosion of the private bargaining process because the parties at the bargaining table would hold back on their best offers until they got to the White House. As I put it, "If the president hangs out his shingle, he'll get all the business."

So I was tested. In the summer of 1968, longshore-
men on the East and Gulf coasts began a strike.
President Johnson enjoined the strike, using
Taft-Hartley authority, declaring that it would create
a national emergency. His decision was appealed on
a fast track directly to the Supreme Court, and the
court agreed with the president. In January 1969,
the injunction period expired and I was sworn in
as secretary of labor. *Okay, Professor:*

Now what are you going to do?

Relying on what I had learned from the world of ideas,
I said to President Nixon, "Your predecessor was
wrong and the Supreme Court was wrong. This strike
will produce turmoil, but it will not lead to a national
emergency. If you bring the dispute to the White House,
you will be spending much of your term in office dealing
with labor disputes. If you hold off that pressure, I will
mediate actively and we will get the strike settled."
The president hung in, we got the strike settled in a
few weeks, and we sent a loud message about the
process of collective bargaining:

The President's shingle is not out there, so solve your problems yourselves.

This was also an important lesson in public life for
me. I found that what I learned in the world of ideas
can be applied to the world of action, but only if
I am willing to fight for the ideas, to let private
processes work themselves out—even if that means
some turmoil—and to act vigorously to deal directly
with any fallout.

Signed photo from I.W. Abel, founder and President of the United Steelworkers. George Meany, President of the AFL-CIO, on the right. George Shultz was Secretary of Labor at the time.

George Shultz (far left) in an Oval Office meeting with President Richard Nixon.

Meeting with Soviet Premier Leonid Brezhnev.

Москва 1973 год.

STRATEGY / A critical lesson from the study of economics is the importance of having a strategy—a sense of long-term consequences. Sound economic policies work, but most often success comes only after the passage of time, or, as economists say, with a lag. Politicians are impatient, so economists have a problem persuading people to wait for results. As I once lamented, "An economist's *lag* can be a politician's *nightmare*."

As director of the Office of Management and Budget in the early 1970s, I fought and lost a battle involving lags. Inflation was a problem. We had the budget under control and, in a speech titled "Steady as You Go," I argued that with a sensible monetary policy in place, inflation would be brought under control.

I lost to impatience. Through a contentious process, wage and price controls were imposed. The immediate result seemed positive, but, as I and others had predicted, the long-term results were disastrous distortions in the economy. This was a frustrating case where I was unable to implement what I had learned in the world of ideas. In the end, a re-imposition of wage and price controls led to my resignation as secretary of the Treasury. But the experience stays with me as I ask myself why so many good ideas are hard to implement and what can be done to improve the process. Sometimes a big, unpleasant surprise—a shock such as *Sputnik*—does the job: *Sputnik* prodded us in the United States and got us going energetically on our own space program, even sending a man to the moon. We have to ask, however: Why do we need a shock to prod us into doing obvious things? Why can't we take clear and resolute action before the shock?

EXECUTION / Students sometimes say, "You have administered in business, in government, and in universities," and then ask, "What is the difference?"

There are different adages that apply, depending on the work setting.

When I went into *business*, I quickly learned that you need to be careful when you tell someone working for you to do something because the chances are high that he or she will do it. In *government*, you don't have to worry about it, and in the *university*, you are not supposed to tell anybody to do anything in the first place.

"NOTHING EVER GETS SETTLED IN THIS TOWN"

The substantive difference involves the different missions of business, government, and academia. Our government has been designed with checks and balances. The idea is that, because issues can have great significance, it is important that they be debated and challenged. As I once remarked when I was in office, "Nothing ever gets settled in this town." The big exception is the military, whose job it is to get the mission done, not to argue. That is why we turn so often to the military in any kind of crisis situation.

Shultz, while Dean of the Graduate School of Business at the University of Chicago.

Talking with students while Dean of the Graduate School of Business at the University of Chicago.

By contrast, universities are all about learning, and their focus is on the individual student. So the basic unit of authority is the individual, which creates a sort of inverted-triangle style of organization instead of the traditional top-down arrangement found in most businesses.

Businesses are, in considerable part, executing organizations. Yes, they set policies and strategies, but their emphasis is on cost-effective performance in a competitive environment. That is what it takes to survive and prosper.

I saw this competitive drive in my time as an executive in the Bechtel Group, which was, and still is, a large engineering and construction company operating on a global basis. It is constantly competing with good companies throughout the world on price, quality, and on-time delivery. Procurement is an important function of business. You have to be an effective buyer in order to compete, and your managerial systems can make a big difference.

Above all, close attention to people is essential. Leadership is critical to success in business, so you need to find good people, hire them, test them, and develop them through a variety of experiences. You'll find out then who can stand up to the inevitable tough situations that will arise.

At Bechtel, I also learned that problems are of different types and therefore they need to be approached in different ways. For example, safety in the workplace is a prime objective at Bechtel. I learned that this is one of those problems that is not solvable in the "done with that" sense. You create a safe workplace by consistent attention to the subject, and you work at it constantly because it is all about attitudes.

These and other insights from my business experience helped me in many ways in public life. Sometimes you do better when you realize that certain problems just have to be worked at—*must* be worked at—if a situation is to be prevented from deteriorating, let alone moved toward resolution. In many ways, this is the nature of the Israeli-Palestinian problem. More on this to come.

AFL-CIO News

American Federation of Labor & Congress of Industrial Organizations
AFL · CIO

Vol. XIV
Issued weekly at
815 Sixteenth St., N. W.
Washington, D. C. 20006
$2 a year

Saturday, March 1, 1969

No.

Second Class Postage Paid at Washington, D. C.

MEETING BETWEEN Labor Sec. George P. Shultz, right, and AFL-CIO Executive Council was described by Federation Pres. George Meany as "constructive" and "cordial." Shultz extended an invitation to the council from Pres. Nixon for a White House meeting.

SECTION 2 /
Civil Rights

I had a riveting experience as co-chairman with Clark Kerr of the Armour Automation Committee, formed in the early 1960s by the unions and management of the Armour Meat Packing Company to address plant-closure issues as the industry was restructuring.

"WE HAVE NO MORE ROOMS"

After the announcement of a plant shutdown in Texas, a team of four of us flew to Fort Worth—my associate, Arnie Weber; a management representative; a labor representative, who was black; and me. We went to the hotel to register and they very politely gave Arnie and me a nice room with twin beds. Then the management representative was given his room. When the labor representative tried to register, he was told there were no more rooms available. He then produced something none of us had, a confirmation slip. The clerk took it to some higher authority. He came back and repeated, "We have no more rooms." By this time, my blood was rising. With a tone of finality, I said, "You gave me a room. Put an extra bed in it. So you *do* have a room." The clerk was flustered, so he did what I practically had ordered him to do. I had experienced discrimination firsthand. It's one thing to read about it and acknowledge it intellectually. It's something else to experience discrimination personally and realize in your gut how ugly and unacceptable it is. I also learned that firmness can pay off.

George Shultz with Walter Reuther, President of the United Auto Workers.

Later, Clark and I, in our mediator-arbitrator role, helped the committee find its way to a bumping agreement, whereby workers with enough seniority in a plant that was being closed could replace junior workers in another plant in a different location if they chose to do so. Not long after that, the company started building a plant in a small town in Minnesota. The town fathers had given concessions to the company in order to bring those good jobs to their town. As that new plan neared completion, the company's large old meat-packing plant in Kansas City was closed. Suddenly we could see there was a likelihood of workers from the now-closed plant exercising the bumping option into the Minnesota plant. Most of the Kansas City workers were black, and we discovered that there were no blacks at all in the Minnesota town. It was the mid-1960s, when tensions were rising, particularly in urban areas. What to do?

We worked with people on both ends. The black employees sent scouting parties from Kansas City to see what the town was like. The town fathers, it turned out, had a lot of civic pride. Big cities don't know how to handle human problems, but we do, they said. Then the churches in town discovered that the potential new residents were tithers, so a competition began among the town's churches to attract them as new parishioners. That was like a welcome mat. In the end, a fair number of black workers moved from Kansas City to Minnesota and, miraculously, the whole thing worked.

I had these examples in mind when I chaired a committee to manage the end of segregation in the schools of seven southern states. Here we were in 1970, long after *Brown v. Board of Education*.

President Nixon had decided that the system of legal segregation would end when the school year started that fall. My job was to figure out how to manage the transition so that the quality of education could be maintained and violence avoided.

My earlier experiences helped me a lot as I worked with soon-to-be Senator Pat Moynihan and White House aide Len Garment on the problem. We recruited biracial committees in each state. We determined not to inquire about anyone's political affiliation. We wanted strong people who were respected. Then, one state group at a time, we brought them to the White House. I remembered a lesson I'd learned from my mediation days: When people argue about matters of principle, you have a hard time finding a compromise, but if you can get them to address tangible problems, you have a chance of finding solutions. I also remembered that firmness can pay off. So in our meetings I let committee members get statements of principle—for integration, for separate schools—off their chests. Then I told them, "The argument you have been having this morning about desirability is obviously important to you, but, beginning this fall, it is irrelevant. The schools will open on an integrated basis; that has been decided. What you really have on your hands are operational problems. How are you going to manage it when the schools open? You all have a stake in the quality of education in your communities." Gradually they pitched in.

As schools opened that fall, there were some tense moments, but in the end there was no violence. The biracial committees had worked the issues skillfully in their communities. Once again, ideas from my experience in the labor relations area paid off.

SECTION 3 /
Human Rights

The search for freedom in all its forms, including political and economic freedom and security, was a motivating imperative for President Reagan. I was with him wholeheartedly in this effort.

"TRANSLATE THE IDEA OF FREEDOM INTO ACTION"

We saw many positive developments in the 1980s: the sweep of democracy in South America—Brazil, Argentina, and, most notably, Chile—and elsewhere, as in the Philippines and South Korea. No effort got more sustained attention than that of improving the lot of Soviet Jews, who were virtually imprisoned in the Soviet Union, and of gaining the opportunity for them to emigrate. Their situation posed a tremendous problem for us as we sought to translate the idea of freedom into action.

OVERLEAF: Ida Nudel with George Shultz.

Ida Nudel, Refusenik, with her dog while in exile in
Kriboshehino, Siberia.

On the morning of October 15, 1987, I was asked to be available for a phone call from Jerusalem. At 3:18 that afternoon, the call came through: "This is Ida Nudel. I'm in Jerusalem. I'm home." My eyes filled with tears, as they still do when I think of that moment. How had this happened and how was it that so many other Soviet Jews were allowed to emigrate?

The courage and ingenuity of the Jews in the Soviet Union were the key ingredients, the necessary condition, for this successful outcome. Their courage also interacted with efforts by others, and that is also part of the story. Aleksandr Kholmiansky, the former "prisoner of Zion" who was sent to a labor camp in 1984 on false charges, recounts:

We [the Jewish activists] knew that our blood had a price and that this price was not insignificant....The mere awareness that somebody was somewhere struggling for us was a highly important feeling for us...it provided us with a sense of protection and immunity, and offered one of the rarest examples of a victory over the KGB. [1]

Two ideas played a big part in the human rights successes of the Reagan era.

---

1 Aleksandr (Ephraim) Kholmiansky, interview by Sarah Fainberg, June 28, 2009, "Friends Abroad: The Moral and Political Significance of the Soviet Jewry Movement for the Jewish Activists within the Soviet Union," in *The Jewish Movement in the Soviet Union*, edited by Yaacov Ro'i, forthcoming.

Ronald Reagan knew that the Soviet Union was "an evil empire," that communism would be relegated to "the ash heap of history," and predicted that the internal failures of the Soviet system would bring about its demise. He saw that change was possible and he worked to bring about that change. I agreed with his thinking and did my utmost to help. At that time, many experts on the Soviet Union scorned the idea that change was possible, so Ronald Reagan's belief was bold, exciting, and motivating, even though it was ridiculed.

In the Reagan era, we inherited a Soviet relationship tied to the concept of linkage—that is, all the issues were tied together. When the Soviets invaded Afghanistan, President Carter was surprised, distressed, and angered. In reaction, he shut down every-thing from U.S. athletes' participation in the Moscow Olympics to consideration by the Senate of an arms control agreement, and even to the annual visit of Foreign Minister Gromyko to Washington prior to the opening of the UN General Assembly.

As I took office, my friend West German Chancellor Helmut Schmidt counseled me: "George, the situation is dangerous; there is no human contact." To put it another way, linkage had been vastly overdone. President Reagan understood how that could work against the right outcome. It could encourage the Soviets to do something bad just so they could agree to give it up in order to get something else in the linkage chain they wanted. And if the Soviets did something good, linkage mentality put pressure on us to overlook something else they were doing wrong. Above all, Ronald Reagan was determined to pursue freedom for Soviet Jewry no matter what else was going on.

I put a lot of store in individual leadership. Senator Henry "Scoop" Jackson had a clear and uncompromising view of the Communist threat. President Ford and Secretary Kissinger were farsighted in recognizing the potential for human rights embodied in the Helsinki Accords. My hero is Ronald Reagan, who put human rights and Soviet Jewry at the top of his agenda.

Leadership mattered on the Soviet side as well. General Secretary Gorbachev and Foreign Minister Shevardnadze were leaders with whom we could have a real conversation. When you combine new ideas, the leverage of Helsinki, and leaders who are convinced that change is possible, then something big can happen.

When I became secretary of state in 1982, Jewish emigration from the Soviet Union virtually had been halted. In 1983, only 1,300 Jews were allowed to emigrate.

As I prepared for my first meeting with Soviet Foreign Minister Andrei Gromyko shortly after taking office in 1982, I focused on human rights practices in the Soviet Union. I assembled lists of people who had been denied permission to emigrate, reviewed the special problems of Soviet Jewry, and expanded my knowledge of the full range of our human rights concerns. After I met with Avital Shcharansky, the intense and compelling wife of the famous dissident, I was wrung out. The woeful treatment of her unjustly imprisoned husband, his courage, and my inability to provide any real assurance about his release made for immense frustration. Avital's pleas dramatized the human side of the tension in U.S.–Soviet relations. "The president and I will never give up on pressing the cause of human rights and the case for your husband's release," I told her.

On October 22, 1984, the National Assembly of the National Conference on Soviet Jewry gave me an award for our efforts. I was honored but embarrassed. We had achieved very little. The situation of Soviet Jews remained, as I'd described, "very grim."

Human rights activists were dying in labor camps and prisons, and the small group of idealists who monitored Soviet compliance with its obligations under the Helsinki Final Act were imprisoned and exiled. Foreign tourists attempting to assist Refuseniks or activists were hounded and sometimes jailed. My friend, the late

Congressman Jim Scheuer of New York, was arrested and imprisoned for participating in a demonstration in Moscow. (He often
expressed his gratitude to the Soviets for the unexpected boost this
gave his political career.)

At the Geneva Summit meeting between President Reagan and
General Secretary Gorbachev in November 1985, we made significant
progress on arms control issues but, more importantly, we changed
the atmosphere of U.S.-Soviet relations. On February 11, 1986,
Anatoly Shcharansky crossed the Glienicke Bridge to West Berlin
as part of a careful deal that carried no implication of his being
a spy. The deal demonstrated that we could bargain successfully
with the new Soviet leadership.

We made another deal under tense circumstances in September 1986
after the Soviets arrested Nicholas Daniloff, a reporter whom they
entrapped to exchange for Gennadi Zakharov, a Soviet scientific
attaché. We secured freedom for Daniloff, freedom for physicist
Yuri Orlov and his wife, and a promise by Shevardnadze that he
would work on getting other dissidents and Refuseniks released.
Zakharov, after a plea of nolo contendere, returned to the Soviet
Union. Shevardnadze followed through over the next year: all the
people on a list we had given him were released or pardoned.

Then came the extraordinary meeting between Ronald Reagan and
Mikhail Gorbachev on October 11-12, 1986, in Reykjavik, Iceland.
While no full agreement was consummated there, great progress
was made on major arms control issues, and the prospect of a world
free of nuclear weapons was seriously discussed. Not so well noticed
was the agreement by the Soviets, achieved in an all-nighter by
Assistant Secretary of State Roz Ridgway, to make human rights a
recognized and regular part of our agenda.

The Glienicke Bridge between East and West Berlin.

Anatoly Shcharansky walking to freedom, February 11, 1986.

On Monday, April 13, 1987, I met Shevardnadze in
Moscow. Specific negotiating groups were formed,
including one on human rights. I sensed greater openness. When I arrived that evening at our ambassador's
residence, Spaso House, everything was ready for
the Passover seder. The elegant ballroom had been
transformed into a warm and welcoming sanctuary.
Dozens of the most famous Jewish Refuseniks were
there. I put on a yarmulke, met them all, and then said
exactly what all of us felt:

You are on our minds; you are in our hearts. We never give up, we
never stop trying, and in the end some good things may happen. But
never give up, never give up. And please note that there are people all
over the world, not just in the United States, who think about you and
wish you well and are on your side.

Their determination amazed me. We held the seder to
encourage them. *But I realized that they had given me far
more strength and resolve than I possibly could have given
them.* In many ways, that is the message of this effort:
the courage of the Refuseniks themselves is the most
important part of the story.

Negotiations with Shevardnadze resumed after the
seder, and I moved the conversation to human rights.
I focused on Shevardnadze's position, as he had
expressed it to me in an earlier meeting, that the Soviets
would change their policies to suit their own interests, not
in response to U.S. pressure or to please us. Speaking
very slowly so his note-taker could write down every
word, I read him a prepared statement on the reasons
why allowing human rights to flourish in the Soviet
Union would "stimulate the creativity and drive of

individuals," which was the key, in the fast-moving information age, to enhanced economic well-being and stability in international affairs. Shevardnadze told me privately in September 1989 that he went over the notes of this meeting "carefully with Gorbachev and others in the leadership," and that what I had said "had a profound impact."

The next day, April 14, 1987, I met with Gorbachev. We were making progress on arms control, and when Gorbachev completed his comments on that subject, he invited me to raise any subject of interest to me. I raised human rights. I thanked him for the progress being made and said we hoped for further moves. He said, "The Soviet side is prepared to consider any proposal that emerges in the humanitarian area," but then attacked me for holding the Passover seder at our embassy the night before. I was stimulating discontent, he said, and dealing with only "a certain group of Jews, people who don't like it here and have complaints," while showing no interest in the millions of other Jews "who are out of your field of vision." I said the only way anyone could know who wants to leave is to give them the right to do so. "Try it," I urged. "I've got a great big airplane. If you don't want [the Refuseniks who were at the seder] … you can just put them all on and get rid of them. We'll take them." He responded by attacking the United States for mistreating its own minorities, but I regarded the exchange as real progress. He was now willing to discuss human rights so long as he created a transcript which showed that he hit back. That was okay with me. By the end of October 1987, I knew the Soviets were in a major shift on Soviet Jewry. By Passover of the following year, 1988, all of the prominent Refuseniks at the seder had been allowed to emigrate.

On October 15, Ida Nudel called me from Israel, where she had just arrived. She was one of the courageous individuals named on a list I had given Shevardnadze in concluding the Daniloff affair. She gave Ronald Reagan and me a lot of credit for the positive developments that were now unmistakably evident. We could not be sure what was causing the changes, but certainly the Soviets had come to believe that it was in their interests to allow emigration.

The problems for Israel in absorbing such a huge wave of Soviet Jews were brought home to me vividly as these events unfolded. Back at my home on the Stanford University campus, I gave a party for a few of my economist friends. We were discussing intently the financial implications of this influx. At one point, Herb Stein, who had worked with me on the successful effort to stabilize Israel's economy in 1986, announced: "Israel just struck oil." He got everyone's attention. Really? Where? How much? "Not *real* oil," he said. "Something even better—Soviet immigrants: engineers, scientists, doctors, musicians, Jewish boys and girls. Human beings. The ultimate resource." He raised his glass, and we drank to that.

Helping save Soviet Jewry was a gratifying achievement. It is worthwhile to examine the tactics that appear to have contributed to it.

The single most important reason for the Soviet Jewish exodus was the determination of the Soviet Jews themselves and of those non-Jews who shared their desire for freedom. Anatoly Shcharansky, his devoted wife Avital, their many colleagues and allies, Andrei Sakharov, every Hebrew teacher, every person jailed, beaten, or punished for reporting violations of human rights—all brought strength and durability to the cause.

At least equally important were the public, even raucous, efforts by American Jews to make the denial of freedom a costly policy. As I said in 1984, "It is not the advocacy of human rights, but rather their denial, that is the source of tension in world affairs." Every form of advocacy had its skeptics, even opponents, among those seeking the same outcome. Yet, in retrospect, we should recognize that it is much easier to live with the charge that we went too far, made too much noise, too much trouble, than to live with the bitter realization after the fact that we did too little. As Elie Wiesel said at the famous December 1987 rally in Washington, D.C.: "Millions of Jews would have been saved" if we had had rallies in the 1940s.

Our commitment to diplomacy was part of a strategy based on strength, including the willingness to use force to defend against aggression. We had no illusion that verbal threats could substitute for real pressure. But at the same time, we believed that change was possible.

◊ First, while we condemned Soviet misconduct, we deliberately abandoned the notion that we would refuse to talk to them if they behaved poorly. Our purpose, after all, was to convince them to alter their behavior. We had our own agenda, which we could not advance if we refused to engage.

◊ We abhorred the actions of the Soviet regime, and we let them know it, but we worked to bring about real change based ultimately on convincing the Soviets that the changes we advocated were in their own best interests.

◊ We curbed our desire to claim small victories in order to encourage larger ones. Instead of taking public credit for Soviet behavior we had encouraged, President Reagan promised not to "crow." It is difficult enough to get leaders of hostile regimes to agree to alter their conduct without making them seem to have capitulated to *our* demands.

The test of successful diplomacy is whether objectives are accomplished. While diplomacy without pressure is idle talk, refusing to talk is no substitute for the pressure essential to elicit change.

Effective diplomacy remains important. Enemies of freedom continue to wield power in the world. We can count on having to face new threats. So the best of all reasons to record and remember how the Soviet Jews were saved is so that we are prepared to act again when the need arises. If we are ever to live in a civilized world, what was accomplished by and for Soviet Jews must become the rule rather than the exception. We must not only preach the doctrine of human rights. We must learn how to be our brother's keeper.

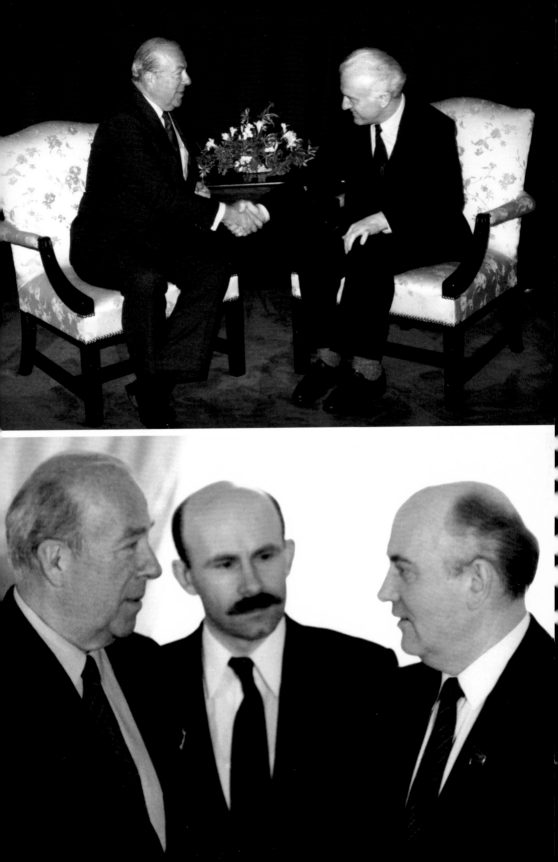

Success in Negotiations: Ten Commandments

Much of what you do in the world of work involves negotiating, and we in the field of labor relations spend a lot of our time studying and practicing this high art. The same is true in diplomacy and in business. Here are some of the things we have learned—and which I have applied. I'll call them

The Ten Commandments for Success in Negotiations.

You will see that my little list is familiar to you because everybody negotiates from time to time, be it in big or small deals. As you are negotiating, you will see some familiar territory that might be labled Negotiations 101. Once again, you will see here the interplay of ideas and action.

George Shultz with Chinese leader Deng Xiaoping.

George Shultz with Soviet Leader Yuri Andropov, while
Foreign Minister Andrei Gromyko looks on (at left).

{1}

BE IN CONTROL OF YOUR CONSTITUENCY / First of all, it is important to remember that the parties at the negotiating table are the tip of the iceberg. They represent the various constituencies, and if you are unaware of that, you can't be a good negotiator. Often the most difficult negotiations occur within constituencies, so commandment number one is to be sure your constituency is solidly behind you.

I used this insight to my advantage many times. As secretary of state, I went to Geneva in January 1985 to negotiate the resumption of arms control talks with the Soviet Union. This was a tense moment and I had detailed instructions from the president, worked out in a laborious process involving all the relevant government agencies. The expectation was that, with these instructions in hand, I would take a small delegation with me. To the consternation of some of my advisers, I took a large delegation so that all of the agencies of government with a strong, legitimate interest in the outcome were ably represented. It was a bit cumbersome, yes, but in the end, everyone was part of the process. I kept everyone informed, and when we settled, everyone was on board. Constituencies matter, so they must be informed and involved.

The same is true when you are negotiating a treaty that will require a two-thirds vote in the Senate for ratification. The senators must be kept informed. As they often reminded me: If you want me with you on the landing, include me on the take-off.

Of course, you're always wondering whether the guy sitting on the other side of the negotiating table has his constituency under control. If not, you are headed for trouble.

Even small incidents can reveal important information. For example, when I was dealing with a new foreign minister of the Soviet Union, Eduard Shevardnadze, I wondered about his relationship with his boss—*his* constituency—Mikhail Gorbachev. I reflected on a previous experience. In his early days as leader of the Soviet Union, Mikhail Gorbachev decided that the Soviet people, especially the Russians, drank too much vodka, so he made it very difficult to get vodka. During a lengthy negotiation in Vienna with Soviet Foreign Minister Gromyko, who was touting Gorbachev's program, I said, "You know, we tried something like that in our country and it didn't work out too well. You have to worry about street humor." I told him about a joke making the rounds in Moscow:

Two guys are standing in line at a vodka store. An hour goes by, then an hour and a half, and they're just inching ahead. Finally, one of them says, "I'm sick of this. I'm going over to the Kremlin to shoot Gorbachev," and he leaves. About a half hour later, he comes back and finds that his buddy is still in line. His buddy looks at him and says, "Well, did you shoot him?" He says, "Hell no. The line over there is a lot longer than this one."

Gromyko did not laugh.

George Shultz and Andrei Gromyko at the Soviet Mission in Geneva, January 7, 1985. "Time flies when you're having fun."

I reflected on this incident as we prepared for the first meeting between President Reagan and General Secretary Gorbachev in Geneva, which was a major event. The protocol of such meetings is intricately planned, and the first dinner was hosted by the Soviets. President Reagan and Nancy, several others, and I sat on one side. On their side were Gorbachev and his wife Raisa, Shevardnadze, and a few others. We sat down for dinner and a waiter passed around a gigantic bowl of caviar. Another waiter poured vodka into our shot glasses. Shevardnadze picked up his glass of vodka and said to President Reagan, "Mr. President, thank God for Geneva. I had to come all this way to get some vodka." He downed his vodka and everyone followed suit and laughed, including Gorbachev. It was a good sign that Gorbachev and Shevardnadze were connected. You can't joke with somebody about a serious issue unless you have a good relationship. Shevardnadze had his constituency under control.

Another example of the importance of constituencies comes from my early tenure as secretary of state. The Europeans had contracted with the Soviet Union for a pipeline to bring gas into Europe. We thought it was a bad idea for the Europeans to be so dependent on the Soviets during the Cold War, and we had many meetings on the issue in which I negotiated with Claude Cheysson, then the foreign minister of France. He was bright, interesting, and engaging, as the French can be. We worked out an agreement but nothing happened. Then President Mitterrand invited me to meet with him in Paris. When I arrived, I looked around the president's office. No Cheysson. He had not been invited to come. From his absence, I learned that, although I enjoyed talking with him, I shouldn't deal with him because he was in no position to deliver the French constituency. Instead, Mitterrand and I worked out a deal that stuck.

{2}

UNDERSTAND THE NEEDS OF THE OTHER SIDE /

When negotiating, it is essential to understand the other side's needs. As I worked hard on human rights issues with the Soviet Union, Foreign Minister Shevardnadze said to me, "George, we might do some of the things you want, but not to please you. We'll only do them if they are to our advantage." I thought long and carefully about that remark. I developed a position paper in the mid-1980s arguing that an information age was sweeping the world, and in such an environment a closed and compartmentalized society would fall behind. I suggested that the Soviet Union should loosen up for its own good. I am not sure how much impact that suggestion had but (as recounted earlier) a subsequent conversation with Shevardnadze suggests that it helped bring about the dramatic change in Soviet attitudes toward issues such as immigration.

PERSONAL FACTORS / Personal relationships are an essential element in negotiations. For example, the friendship that Shevardnadze and I developed had a positive impact on our negotiations. Personal relationships can help prevent unnecessary problems, and they sometimes make it possible to convey something important and have it believed.

An example comes from a U.S.–Soviet negotiating session in Washington that included a little sub-group that was focused on Afghanistan. The Soviets had invaded the country in 1979 and we wanted them out. Before the predictably rancorous discussion began, Shevardnadze asked to see me alone. We went into a side office with our interpreters and he said, "We are going to go through familiar arguments out there, but I want you to know that we have decided to leave Afghanistan. There will be no immediate announcement, but we've made the decision; it's behind us. We want to get out by the end of 1988. How the United States acts will make a difference because the quicker we're out, the less blood will be shed." Most people in our administration dismissed this but, because of our good past experiences with Shevardnadze, President Reagan and I believed him. On that basis, we managed to maneuver in such a way that the Soviets left Afghanistan sooner than anyone had expected and much bloodshed was avoided as a result.

So personal factors can make a difference, but they should not be given too much weight. Getting to know your opposite number can be helpful, but do not expect to persuade the other person to go against his or her constituency on the basis of personal friendship with *you*. Attempts to defy their constituency would be ill-advised, dangerous, and therefore highly unlikely.

{4}

AN EDUCATIONAL PROCESS / Another commandment is to accept negotiating as an educational process. Most constituencies include members who will make many extreme demands. You learn, and you must lead your constituency to learn, how difficult, if not impossible, it is to achieve what some hard-line group may want. You have to give your constituency time to get used to that, and, at the same time, educate yourself. As a good negotiator, you must try constantly to determine what is really important to the other side and what is less important. That will inform you where the likely trades are. It's an educational process and you have to take the time to let things settle in that way.

Sometimes you have to educate your opposite number about the strength of conviction of your own constituency. When the Soviets seized U.S. reporter Nicholas Daniloff in August of 1986 and accused him of being a spy, they created tremendous tension in the U.S.–Soviet relationship. Feelings ran high. They had framed Daniloff, and had done so skillfully. He was not guilty, but he was in real trouble. Shevardnadze came to the United States to negotiate the matter and I wanted him to understand how strongly President Reagan felt about it. It was arranged with President Reagan that at some point in my conversation with Shevardnadze, I would say, "Let's go over to the White House and see President Reagan." When we arrived, President Reagan, who usually had a pleasant demeanor, was severe. He expressed his views forcefully and allowed no discussion. Shevardnadze got the message, and that message contributed to Daniloff's release.

Nicholas Daniloff after being freed by the Soviets.

AN ONGOING PROCESS / It is important to remember when negotiating a particular issue that it isn't the last negotiation you'll be doing with your opposite number: it is likely that you will have a continuing relationship. In a labor–management deal, you will keep working with your counterparts over time. You want to be sure that the lessons that people take away from the negotiating process are good ones.

In the atmosphere of many strikes in the late 1940s and 1950s, some thoughtful labor and management leaders recognized that there were numerous examples of constructive relationships. They launched a project to have case studies written on the theme of "The Causes of Industrial Peace Under Collective Bargaining," and I wrote two of those case studies. As time passed, we noticed that in quite a few cases the relationship had deteriorated. The reason always seemed the same: the parties had come to value their relationship too much. When problems arose on either side, the answer always seemed to be: We've got a great thing going here; don't rock the boat. After some time, the relationship deteriorated because it no longer served the interests of the people in it.

When I took office as secretary of state, I found that our relationship with China was strained. As I dug in, it seemed to me that the problem resembled one I had seen before. The old China hands who dominated the picture were preoccupied with the relationship. The Chinese are skillful negotiators and they realized and used this preoccupation, saying: If you do such and such, that will damage the relationship, or, if you don't do this, we'll go downhill. The result was that we did not pay enough attention to the substantive issues involved and no real progress toward our objectives was being made.

I talked this over with President Reagan. As president of the Screen Actors Guild in the 1940s and 1950s, he had negotiated on behalf of the union, so he saw the point right away. We set about changing our approach. We made it clear that we were there to talk about problems and opportunities. The Chinese responded well. We set up an agenda and scheduled regular meetings to work through the issues. Gradually, the relationship became constructive as we emphasized the substantive interests of both countries rather than the maintenance of friendship.

With Deng Xiaoping in the Great Hall of the People, Beijing, July 15, 1988.

Awakened in the pre-dawn hours, Bud McFarlane and George Shultz discuss the ominous situation in Grenada with President Reagan, Augusta, Georgia, October 22, 1983.

{6}

CREDIBILITY / Credibility is another fundamental element in negotiations. To remain credible in the eyes of the world, a president must do what he says he's going to do. I remember telling President Reagan a story with a moral that we both tried to observe. When I was in Marine Corps boot camp at the start of World War II, my sergeant handed me my rifle and said, "This is your best friend, so take good care of it. And remember: Never point this rifle at anyone unless you are willing to pull the trigger." Empty threats undermine your credibility, so be careful with your words.

When President Reagan took on the air-traffic controllers in 1981, it was a big event that was watched all over the world. Every country knows that if you bring down the air-traffic system within a country, flights will be affected worldwide. This can be devastating, so the controllers have inherent power. A president who says, "You're fired" must seem foolish, but there was Reagan issuing an order to terminate them. And there were the controllers, who had taken an oath under the Constitution that they would not strike, yet they did. Advisers said, "Mr. President, this is a very complicated situation." His retort was, "It's not complicated. It's simple. They took an oath, they violated the oath. They're out. It's simple." So what happened to the air-traffic system? The president was lucky. He had had the foresight

12 Part I/Friday, August 7, 1981 Los Angeles T[imes]

Reagan Action Toughest in History

BARBARA MARTIN / Los Angeles Times

Charles Bradshaw, a traffic controller at Palomar Airport for seven years, hugs his son Phillip while holding in his left hand a restraining order served on him at Lindbergh Field's east terminal.

Called Bid to Reverse Tolerant Attitude on Illegal Walkouts

By WILLIAM J. EATON, *Times Staff Writer*

WASHINGTON—President Reagan's decision to fire all 12,000 defiant air traffic controllers and deny them amnesty is the toughest action ever taken by a U.S. President against striking federal employees.

And the dismissal of virtually an entire work force, coupled with Reagan's avowed refusal to permit reinstatement of defiant strikers under any circumstance, are a dramatic bid to reverse the relatively tolerant attitude toward illegal walkouts by public employees that has developed in this country in recent years.

As such, the President's stance on the controllers' strike may be the labor relations equivalent of his all-out fight for budget and tax cuts—a bold attempt to reshape prevailing patterns of public policy and return them to what he sees as the tougher, less permissive standards of earlier times.

'Total Capitulation'

"It's the most serious confrontation in the history of public employee bargaining relations," said Theodore W. Kheel, a New York mediator and arbitrator with 40 years of experience at the bargaining table. "I have never known a situation of this magnitude where the door is closed to discussion. Once you say you won't talk, there's nothing left but total capitulation."

Reagan's action is not without its costs. In effect, he is sacrificing an experienced work force whose training is valued at $525 million, and there will be heavy additional expenses for the schooling of replacements. In the meantime, the air traffic system will not be operating normally for months, perhaps for a year or more.

But the President has sent a stern warning to other federal workers about the consequences of illegal strikes and the message may strengthen the hand of state and city officials faced with unlawful walkouts by their public employee unions.

Former Secretary of Labor George P. Shultz defended Reagan's actions, saying that the chief executive had no choice but to uphold the law.

"The President might well be thinking that there's only one thing worse than an illegal strike and that's a successful illegal strike," said Shultz, a former specialist in industrial relations and now president of Bechtel Inc.

When Shultz was chief labor adviser to President Richard M. Nixon in 1970, however, there was no similar crackdown when 152,000 postal workers walked off the job despite the federal ban on such strikes. Although the Nixon Administration refused to negotiate until the postal strikers went back to work, it took no action to penalize them and granted a pay raise and bargaining rights in the subsequent contract talks.

Similarly, the federal reprisals were slight when 3,000 members of the Professional Air Traffic Controllers Organization struck in 1970 over a three-week period. About 1,000 were suspended, resulting in loss of some pay, and 52 were fired. Two years later, however, 46 of the 52 ousted controllers were rehired.

In a 1978 strike by some postal workers in California and New Jersey, Postmaster General William F. Bolger took a harder line. A total of 226 strikers were fired, although 96 were later reinstated.

In directing the dismissal of every air traffic controller who joined the current strike, however, Reagan has taken an extremely tough position. Labor union officials called Reagan's decision "brutal overkill."

Certainly, there has been no comparable action by any President since Harry S. Truman went to Congress in 1946, during a nationwide railroad strike, and sought legislation to allow him to draft the strikers into the Army.

The railroad strike was settled even as Truman was addressing a joint session of the Senate and House. The House approved the Truman plan 306 to 13 anyway, in less than two hours. The bill died in the Senate, however.

In the current air controllers' strike, some labor analysts contend that the union seems to have a death wish, in view of Reagan's plain warnings that he would seek the dismissal and the prosecu[tion of] strikers. But, the analysts a[...] President shut off any escap[e] or safety valve by refusing [...] further and denying amnesty [...] vance.

"They (the union cont[...]) threw the gauntlet down a[nd the] President threw it back at th[em ...] they both look like ama[...]," Kheel said. In past labor-m[anage]ment crises, he recalled, som[e face-]saving device for one or bot[h sides] normally has been employe[d to] solve a seemingly irreco[ncilable] dispute.

"Now, the President's [...] win," Kheel said. "If he has [to take] back the 12,000 people, he'[...] He's got to destroy the union[...]"

European Controllers May Refuse to Service U.S. Craf[t]

LONDON (AP)—Two leaders of a 60-nation association of air c[on]trollers' unions said Thursday that their members have been ask[ed] to consider refusing to serve U.S.-registered aircraft and to s[top] clearing any planes on flights to the United States.

Ted Bradshaw, one of five board members of the Internatio[nal] Federation of Air Traffic Controller Assns., issued a statement [in] London on behalf of the associations' executive board calling [on] unions in member nations to "consider refusing air traffic con[trol] services to U.S.-registered airplanes."

In Edmonton, Canada, federation President Harri Henschler s[aid] the group also is asking member associations not to clear plane[s of] any nationality across U.S. borders out of concern for the safety [of] American skies.

Bradshaw said there was unanimous support for the strikers a[nd] "every member in Europe is firmly behind some form of action" [to] support them.

British Law 'Vastly Different'

The Italian controllers' union said its members would stag[e a] "work-to-rule" action, strictly following regulations, to "under[line] their opposition to the unjustifiable actions of the American gove[rn]ment and their support of the right to strike."

The action, which began Thursday afternoon, had no immed[iate] effect on Italy's air traffic.

British air traffic controllers reacted angrily to the firing of t[heir] striking colleagues in the United States and one union official [said] the British controllers would carefully consider any request [for] support from the U.S. controllers. "We are entirely behind them [in] this dispute." There was no indication of what form the supp[ort] could take.

"Sorry, this is not the practice a 20th-Century nation should [in]dulge in," said Doug Bush, of the Institute of Professional Civil S[er]vants, representing Britain's 1,500 most senior air traffic cont[rol]lers.

TOWER: Non-Strikers Disagree on Air Safety

Continued from First Page

its AFL-CIO affiliates, would give the controllers a boost that could halt most deliveries to Lindberg Field.

The labor council will supply 150 pickets, who will appear with 50 striking controllers today at an 11 a.m. airport demonstration that will be the controllers' largest show of force to date.

Fight With Government

"This has become more than a fight between (the controllers' union) and the government," said Bruce Travis, the local union president. "It has become a fight between organized labor and government."

Strikers' morale continued high in San Diego, even though most of the strikers said they knew they already had been fired by the government and probably would have to look for new jobs.

"My life's going to take a big change," said striking controller Ken Forrest. "But we're very principled people."

Federal Aviation Administration officials have stressed that air travel throughout the country is safe despite the strike. "Our main interest is safety," Garvis said. "We have only fully qualified controllers directing (air) traffic."

But at least some of those controllers concede that they are dead tired from five straight days of 10-hour shifts and are just plain worried about the busy weekend ahead.

"Let's just say I wouldn't fly any place this weekend," said one Los Angeles-area controller who, like most still on the job, said he was afraid of allowing his name to be used for fear of reprisal.

"I don't think we can go like this for long. I think this weekend will be the acid test. Right now I'm working eight hours a day, six days a week—I'm exhausted."

"It's not safe to fly right now," said Evan Black of Atlanta, a member of the Professional Air Traffic Controllers Organization who stayed on the job at his Georgia post.

"The system functioned very well the first day but unfortunately things have deteriorated the past three days and it's not nearly as safe as the pilots and the FAA are saying it is."

However, one replacement worker who said he had spent 16 years at Los Angeles International Airport before being called back this week from an office job, laughed off contentions that air travel in the Los Angeles area may be unsafe.

"Directing air traffic is like riding a bicycle or making love," he said. "You might get a little rusty if you don't do it for a while but you don't forget."

Throughout the country, control towers have been continuing to function with skeletal crews of non-striking controllers and supervisors. Thirty military air controllers were brought in earlier this week for training at Los Angeles International Airport. But they are not expected to take over critical seats actually directing traffic. One source said they are spending part of their training time this week learning to recognize various commercial airliners.

POLI: Sardonic Humor During Grim Momen[t]

Continued from First Page

At least some of Poli's striking troops appear equally dedicated to him. This was evident Thursday as a sober-faced Poli strode into the Fairfax County, Va., jail to visit one of his imprisoned controllers, Steve Wallaert, of Norfolk, Va., who began a 60-day sentence Wednesday for contempt of court.

"How are you, brother?" Poli asked, embracing him.

"I'm tired, Bob," Wallaert said. "I've had some weak moments. But I'm proud to be a PATCO member—and going to jail was something every PATCO member knew might happen to him."

"They can put our people in shackles, they can put our people in jail," Poli said. "We will not go back to work."

Wallaert, head of a local controllers' union, nodded in agreement. "I'm here till I tell my people to go back to work," he said. "And I'm not going to do that till Bob Poli tells me to."

Former Air Controller

The man who inspired Wallaert's loyalty is a former air traffic controller, a native of Pittsburgh who began his career as a controller there after a stint in the Air Force and later worked in Cleveland. He became executive vice president of the union in 1973.

He took over the presidency early last year after he and former union President John Leyden both resigned in a policy dispute over whether the union was militant enough.

Poli maintained that the union's previous tactics—slowdowns, sick-outs and wildcat strikes—were not adequate. The executive board of the union refused to accept his resignation and made him interim president. He was elected to a full three-year term in April, 1980.

"He really cares for his members," David Trick, the union's director of operations, said. "When people get sick, he sends flowers. He calls their wives. He's that kind of guy."

Trick described Poli as a man of fierce determination who derives much of his resolve from the support of the rank-and-file. "When the whole world is attacking you," Trick said, "you've just got to sit back and say: 'My members are with me.' I have seen him, at times, go into a room by himself and sit, and concentrate, and force himself to relax, to get back to the basic issues in his mind."

Has a Quick Temper

Trick said his boss has a quick temper as well as a sense of humor. "Did you ever meet an Italian in your life who didn't?" Trick asked. "He has to fight constantly to con[trol his]

AP

Robert Poli, the president of the striking air controllers unio[n ...] Steven Wallaert, a local union leader who was jailed in [...]

lip to keep from saying some of those things he'd really like to say."

doubt he's gotten two hours of sleep a night since this starte[d ...]

Kirkpatrick, 31, a travel ag[...]

LEWIS: Effective in Business and Politics

Continued from First Page

headed into another problem such as he faced in the Azores—but this time on a grand scale. He may have to replace thousands of the country's air traffic controllers.

In his first six months in Washington, the transportation secretary has established a reputation as one of the most effective members of the Reagan Cabinet. But he has raised concerns among automobile safety activists such as Ralph Nader and among experts who shudder at any inkling of protectionism in U.S. trade policy.

Nader has viewed Lewis as too willing to roll back automobile safety standards, and some in the trade field see him as too willing to erect barriers to protect Detroit from Japanese auto imports.

Threw Self Into Fight

When the air traffic controllers went to the mat with

mary campaign in Pennsylvania and then moved on to become deputy national campaign manager and, later, deputy chairman of the Republican National Committee.

It was no surprise when he was named transportation secretary.

Lewis is a strikingly handsome man. He is a graduate of Haverford College and the Harvard School of Business, and he still thinks of himself more as a businessman and manager than as a politician, although he has been a power broker in Pennsylvania Republican politics for years and ran unsuccessfully for governor in 1974.

Los Angeles Times article on the firing of air-traffic controllers.

to appoint a secretary of transportation, Drew Lewis, who knew what he was doing. Drew kept the system in operation. All over the world people said, "Reagan must be crazy," but he won. The planes kept flying and those who violated their oath were out of a job. With this win, Reagan gained credibility.

In 1983, the Soviets, using Cuban nationals, took over the Caribbean island of Grenada and started building an airfield. They also challenged the safety of some 300 American students there. We asked permission to send a ship to take them off the island. Denied. *An airplane or two?* Denied. So we used military force to take the island. It was a clean operation. We went in, brought our people back to the United States, restored the prior government to office, and got out in about two months. For the first time since the Vietnam War, the United States had used military force. The United States had gigantic military capability but people discounted it. They said, "You're afraid to use it," but Reagan used military force in a quick and competent way. Once again, he gained credibility. As a result, when he expressed a point of view, this president's words were listened to with care and taken seriously.

{7}

TIMING / What about timing? Knowing when to push negotiations is of critical importance. If you try to negotiate before you develop a strong hand, you may press for action at the wrong time. The danger is not simply that you may fail; you risk throwing the whole situation off track. Then, it is not just a matter of picking yourself up and starting over again; you will have to begin by first making up for lost ground.

The flow of negotiations with the Soviet Union on nuclear arms is a clear example of the relationship between strength and timing. President Reagan made bold proposals early in his administration. The Soviet Union had around 1,800 intermediate-range nuclear missiles aimed at European targets, and we had none, but we had a NATO-approved plan to start some deployments in Britain, Italy, and Germany if negotiations did not produce an agreement. The president proposed a negotiation with the objective of eliminating completely the weapons we planned and those deployed by the Soviets. He also proposed that strategic weapons be cut in half.

At the time, we were struggling with inflation, our economy was in recession, and our military strength was in the process of being rebuilt. The Soviet objective in the INF negotiations was to prevent any deployment, as envisioned in the NATO plan. They used intimidation and threats against the Europeans. We made new proposals. Their tactics were prisoner to their strategy, so they appeared intransigent while we appeared reasonable. When the Soviets shot down a Korean airliner in September 1983, we led the charge in denouncing this brutal act but sent our negotiators back to Geneva. We would not be bound by the concept of linkage. We consulted carefully at every step with our European allies while they watched the negotiating process closely.

With no success in the negotiations as 1983 came to an end, we proceeded with our scheduled deployments, first in England and then in Italy. In each case, the Soviets stirred the pot but the resulting protests did not succeed in blocking the deployments. The most difficult and contentious deployment was that of ballistic missiles in Germany. The propaganda war by the Soviet Union was fierce, but the deployments proceeded. Our careful and well-known consultations with our European allies and our clear reasonableness as negotiators paid off. The Soviets walked out of negotiations. Times were tense.

As we moved into 1984, our economy was expanding once again, inflation was under control, our military forces were strong, and the deployments—a severe test of NATO cohesion and determination— were behind us. By summer, I was able to tell the president that our diplomats had been approached by their Soviet counterparts in several capitals. Their implicit message was that Soviet Minister Gromyko would welcome an invitation to Washington when he came to attend the UN General Assembly meeting in New York in September. In effect, the Soviets blinked. The meeting took place and it was a major breakthrough.

Against this background and the landslide reelection of President Reagan, I went to Geneva in January 1985 and negotiated an agreement with Gromyko to resume arms control talks. The formal negotiations moved slowly, but when President Reagan and I sat down with General Secretary Gorbachev and Foreign Minister Eduard Shevardnadze in Reykjavik in October 1986, we were pleased that Gorbachev put on the table what President Reagan had proposed at the beginning of his presidency. The time was right at the Reykjavik meeting, and subsequently both of these agreements, the Intermediate-Range Nuclear Forces Treaty (INF) and the Strategic Arms Reduction Treaty (START), were agreed to and put into effect.

At Leonid Brezhnev's funeral, November, 1982.

President Ronald Reagan with Soviet Foreign Minister Andrei Gromyko.

George Shultz showing the Great Seal of the Republic at an Air Force
Association event in September of 1988.

STRENGTH AND DIPLOMACY GO TOGETHER /

To succeed in negotiations, you must bring strength to the table or you will have your head handed to you. As secretary of state, I knew that strength and diplomacy are not alternatives; rather, they complement one another.

The complementary nature of strength and diplomacy is symbolized in the Great Seal of the Republic. It shows an eagle holding an olive branch in one talon and thirteen arrows in the other. After the end of World War II, President Truman saw a variation of the seal in the White House in which the eagle was looking at the arrows. He decreed in an executive order that henceforth the eagle would always look at the olive branch to show that the United States will always seek peace, but it also would hold on to the arrows to show that the United States understands that you must be strong to be effective in seeking peace.

Consider what happened in the Middle East in 2000. President Clinton, approaching the end of his presidency, pressed the Israeli and Palestinian parties to come to Camp David, a place I have had the privilege of visiting many times. Of course, it's where President Sadat and Prime Minister Begin negotiated the agreement leading to the peace treaty between Egypt and Israel. There's a magical quality to Camp David.

Israeli Prime Minister Ehud Barak, U.S. President Bill Clinton, and Palestinian Authority Chairman Yasser Arafat at Camp David, July 2000.

Secluded and quiet, it is an ideal setting for negotiations, yet the magic worked only because both Sadat and Begin brought strength to the table and could speak for and deliver their constituencies.

But in 2000, Prime Minister Barak of Israel was struggling to keep his governing coalition together. He had courageously declared at the beginning of his term as prime minister that he would make serious moves for peace. He had withdrawn Israeli forces from southern Lebanon—a move that was long overdue, but one that suggested weakness. He offered Syria what they had hinted they wanted—negotiations about the Golan Heights—yet they declined. He reached out to the Palestinians and, though he did not get very far, he made it clear he was ready to deal. Now, if you were looking from the other side, what would you think about his constituency? What would you make of it when you saw that his own foreign minister refused to accompany him to Camp David? You would think, Wait a minute, this man really seeks a peace agreement and may make a lot of concessions, but is he able to carry them out? Has he got his country behind him? If you are the mediator trying to help antagonists reach a lasting agreement, you must pay attention to signs like these.

Then there was Yasser Arafat. He was constantly looking over his shoulder at extremist Palestinian groups and other radical Arabs who insisted on nothing short of the destruction of Israel, so he had no constituency for a negotiation. People are constantly saying that Israel must make moves for peace, but without a real negotiating partner, the prospects are dim. Arafat actually said before the meeting started that he could not imagine anything that could be offered to him that he could accept.

What happened? At Camp David, the Palestinians were offered 95 percent of the West Bank and a chunk of Jerusalem; they said no. The message of that refusal was devastating to the Israelis, particularly those who advocated accommodation as the way to achieve peace. Now they must ask themselves whether Israel has any reasonable negotiating partner. In many ways, it is also a devastating message to Palestinians—both those whose desires and aspirations are compatible with the existence of a secure Israel and those living in other Arab lands who have been encouraged to believe that one day they will be able to pour back into Israel, something that is not going to happen. The result? An eruption of violence known as the Second Intifada.

This tense Israeli–Palestinian problem may require a slower process. Some things that are accepted today were said to be completely impossible and unacceptable twenty years ago. A basic lesson may well be that if the process is rushed, you risk running it right off the rails. When leaders who lack the strength to back up their positions are brought together for the give-and-take of negotiations, failure is virtually inevitable.

Delivering a speech at Yad Vashem, the Holocaust Memorial, on May 10, 1985.

George Shultz with Soviet Ambassador Anatoly Dobrynin.

{9}

TRUST IS THE COIN OF THE REALM / A negotiator must be trusted to stand by his word. Ronald Reagan's reputation for keeping his promises was an essential factor in his successful negotiations.

A story that illustrates the importance of trust began with an unexpected snowstorm that kept President Reagan and Nancy in Washington. They invited my wife and me to the White House for an informal supper, during which the president talked about his interest in direct personal contact with the Soviet leadership. I arranged a meeting between him and the Soviet ambassador, Anatoly Dobrynin, the following Tuesday. As they discussed a full range of issues, Ronald Reagan made it clear that the human rights issue was at the top of his agenda. He pointed to the Pentecostals taking refuge in our embassy in Moscow as a glaring illustration of the problem and said, "Let them emigrate. You won't hear any crowing from me." Dobrynin and I made this our special project and we eventually succeeded. When sixty Pentecostals were allowed to leave the Soviet Union for Israel, Ronald Reagan did not crow. So our first negotiation with the Soviets was on human rights, and President Reagan kept his word. Despite great political temptation to do so, he never boasted about the success of this deal, so the Soviets learned that he could be trusted.

President Ronald Reagan carrying a wreath at Bitburg, May 5, 1985.

Reagan's insistence on keeping his word was demonstrated dra-
matically during a presidential visit to Germany. I recall vividly
how, in a session in the Oval Office, Chancellor Helmut Kohl of
West Germany invited President Reagan to visit a cemetery in
Germany where American and German soldiers were buried.
Kohl had done that to good effect with President Mitterrand
of France. The visit would symbolize reconciliation between
our countries, and President Reagan readily agreed. Then the
Germans told us that they had selected the Bitburg Cemetery for
the visit. A storm broke when the press uncovered the fact that
many of the German graves there were those of S.S. officers.
Images of the Holocaust came vividly to the fore. We asked to
change the visit to a different cemetery, but for reasons that were
unfathomable to us, Kohl insisted on Bitburg. President Reagan
had given his word, so he went. Leaders of some other countries
later told me that they were astounded that Reagan had followed
through. He paid a political price, but they all acknowledged that
Reagan was a man who kept his word, even under pressure.

Addressing the General Assembly on the fortieth anniversary of the United Nations, September 23, 1985.

{10}

REALISTIC GOALS / Negotiators will benefit from observing the first nine commandments, but they will require something more before achieving success at the bargaining table.

Sometimes you aim for a major settlement, but there are other times when realism dictates a more modest set of arrangements. What may be needed is simply something that can work for the near future. Everyone can think of situations where they might say, "I can live with that as long as I don't have to agree to it, but if you make me agree to it, I won't be able to live with it." For example, if you can get the violence to stop in the Israeli–Palestinian dispute and get some sort of holding regime in place, then an energetic effort could be made to improve the quality of life of the Palestinian people. Outsiders point to the need to restore trust, a most difficult task, but you can restore hope by identifying ways to improve their quality of life. There are many examples, with water being the most prominent one. Much can be done to increase the supply of water in an area where it is scarce and is therefore a dominant concern. You can do many other things to help, such as improving infrastructure and education. By doing so, you increase hope and enhance the prospects that a less ambitious but practical agreement can hold for a while. And if it holds for a time, then enough confidence may be established to develop the agreement further. With this foundation, it may be possible to build the institutions of security, finance, and governance that can make statehood a reality, achieved not from the top down but from the bottom up.

Nevertheless, I know how difficult this problem is because I struggled with it for years. I worked at it even though the probability of success was low because it always seemed to me that if nothing was being done the process would regress. But if you had some balls in the air—some things that people could at least discuss— then you could avoid moving backward and maybe inch forward slightly. Toward the end of one of my efforts to improve the peace prospects in the Middle East, the difficulties showed up in a cartoon that ran in the *Jerusalem Post*. The cartoon shows a document on the ground labeled "Shultz's Peace Efforts," and I am depicted fending off blows from an Israeli, a Palestinian, and a Jordanian. The caption reads, "Well, at least they agree on something!"

WELL, AT LEAST THEY AGREE ON SOMETHING!

SHULTZ'S PEACE EFFORTS

6/2 for Sec George Shultz

SECTION 5 /
A World Free of Nuclear Weapons

I have left office but I am still involved with issues of public policy. In recent years I have been working hard to transform another major idea into reality. Sid Drell, William Perry, Henry Kissinger, Sam Nunn, and I, along with an increasing number of other major figures in the world, are trying to get action on the steps required to achieve a world free of nuclear weapons.

This objective has been on my mind since my service as a Marine in World War II. I was on a troop ship returning to the United States after two and a half years fighting the Japanese in the Pacific. We knew that we were to be formed into the combat units that would assault the Japanese homeland. Every Marine on the ship had been on at least one landing, so we all had a grim sense of what awaited us. Then we received word that an atomic bomb had been dropped, and then another. None of us had any idea what these bombs were, but we knew they must be important. By the time we made port in San Diego, the war was over. How could we help but put two and two together? The atomic bombs had saved the lives of many of us on that ship.

Then I saw pictures of the devastation of Hiroshima. I was stunned, appalled.

Like everyone living in the Cold War days, I had the threat of a nuclear holocaust at the back of my mind. When I became secretary of state in 1982, I considered the issues posed by nuclear weapons to be among the most urgent problems facing the United States.

Marine George Shultz (on left) in the Palau Islands during World War II.

Reykjavik Summit, October 1986.

Secretary George Shultz, Senator Sam Nunn, and Secretary William Perry at a panel discussion following the premiere of *Nuclear Tipping Point* at Universal Studios, Los Angeles, on January 27, 2010.

President Reagan was determined to reduce drastically the numbers of nuclear weapons until they were finally eliminated altogether. I shared his view and wrote in an article in the Spring 1985 issue of *Foreign Affairs*, "A world free of nuclear arms is an ultimate objective to which we, the Soviet Union, and all other nations can agree."

The summit meeting between President Reagan and General Secretary Gorbachev in Reykjavik, Iceland, in October 1986 produced dramatic results. I well remember sitting alongside President Reagan for two days in a small room where the negotiations took place. Even though the meeting did not finally come to closure, huge reductions in nuclear weapons were put on the table and the two leaders agreed that nuclear weapons should be eliminated entirely. The immediate general reaction around the world was negative, as the conventional wisdom was that the threat of nuclear weapons deterred aggression and kept the peace. Nevertheless, twenty years later nuclear arsenals were one-third or less of what they had been at the time of the Reykjavik Summit.

One of my colleagues at the Hoover Institution, Sid Drell, a physicist, and I decided to hold a conference on the twentieth anniversary of the Reykjavik Summit to discuss the implications of what took place there. We were joined by our colleague at Stanford, former secretary of defense William Perry, and others. One result of that conference was an essay calling for a world free of nuclear weapons and identifying steps to be taken toward that goal. It was published in the *Wall Street Journal* on January 4, 2007, and signed by four well-known Cold Warriors. Perry and I were joined by Henry Kissinger and Sam Nunn, and we have become known as the "Four Horsemen."

The impact around the world has been dramatic. We have held additional conferences, taken part in meetings in Oslo and Rome hosted by the governments of Norway and Italy, published two additional essays in the *Wall Street Journal*, and have been joined in this effort by many others all over the world. Both candidates in the 2008 U.S. presidential campaign endorsed our work and have strongly reaffirmed their support since the election. In September 2009, President Obama chaired a meeting of the UN Security Council at which Resolution 1887, which calls for a world free of nuclear weapons, was adopted unanimously.

Progress has been breathtaking, but the most difficult work lies ahead. In our initial *Wall Street Journal* essay, we wrote, "Without the bold vision, the actions will not be perceived as fair or urgent. Without the actions, the vision will not be perceived as realistic or possible." Once again we see the interplay of ideas and action. Difficulties are apparent, as shown by the nuclear ambitions of Iran and North Korea, but the effort progresses. Of all the projects that I now work on, none comes close to the importance of this issue. We are at a nuclear tipping point and we must succeed in turning the vision of a world free of nuclear weapons into a reality.

/ / /

Receiving the Medal of Freedom, January 19, 1989.

The "Four Horsemen": Henry Kissinger, George Shultz, Sam Nunn, and William Perry.

Former Senator Sam Nunn
Co-Chairman, Nuclear Threat Initiative

on "A World Free of Nuclear Weapons"

Over the past four decades, I have seen George Shultz operate from several sides of the negotiating table. George was a firm and principled arms control negotiator with his Soviet counterparts in Geneva during the Reagan era, where he pressed what many thought an untenable position—the "zero" option on intermediate-range nuclear forces—into a landmark treaty that eliminated an entire class of nuclear weapons. Congressional support and Senate ratification of INF was not a coincidence, because George and his team kept Congress informed and involved every step of the way. At home, George was equally principled and effective pressing for congressional support for President Reagan's arms control policies and defense programs. In every negotiation or discussion, there is one constant with George: his personal and professional integrity, which you can always take to the bank.

Today, George is at the center of a global effort to reassert the vision of a world free of nuclear weapons and pursue practical steps toward that goal—an exercise in leadership that holds the promise of bending the course of history and leading to a safer world. I don't know of anyone but George who could have brought together Democrats and Republicans in America—and a diverse set of his peers abroad—in support of this nonpartisan initiative. George Shultz was—and continues to be—an outstanding diplomat and one of our nation's most respected public servants.

Sid Drell
Senior Fellow, Hoover Institution
Emeritus Professor of Physics, Stanford University

on "A World Free of Nuclear Weapons"

When George Shultz returned to Stanford in 1989 at the end of
the Reagan administration, after a distinguished public career that
spanned four decades, it was certainly not to retire. He moved from
the world of action as a public servant and statesman who was uni-
versally admired and respected for his wisdom and integrity to one
of ideas. As is evident in his essay, ideas and action based upon solid
principle are the key nourishment of his life.

At Stanford he reached out to colleagues in many disciplines, including even physics. He was once again an eager student seeking to
learn. As a consequence, and to my great fortune, this is how we
first met. Our far-ranging conversations touched on many issues of
science and society, with particular emphasis on arms control and
nuclear weapons. These were issues he had devoted much effort
to as secretary of state and that I have been grappling with in their
technical dimensions for many years. We shared growing concerns
that, as the world entered the twenty-first century, a more perilous
era of nuclear proliferation was fast approaching due to the spread of
nuclear know-how and technology.

It was almost inevitable that in the search for new ideas to meet this
challenge, the remarkable summit meeting between Ronald Reagan
and Mikhail Gorbachev in Reykjavik in 1986 would come to mind. On

that occasion, Reagan, together with George at his side urging him on, and Gorbachev made a serious effort to reach an agreement to rid the world of all nuclear weapons.

Unfortunately, they faced too many obstacles of the Cold War at that time and were unable to close the deal on what George has since described as "the highest stakes poker game ever played." Disappointment and frustration at this failure were written all over their faces as the leaders emerged at the conclusion of the meeting. However, the leaders of the United States and the (then) Soviet Union, who possessed approximately 98 percent of all the world's nuclear weapons, had agreed to start reducing their bloated arsenals. This was new and important.

The memories of Reykjavik remained very much on George's mind and provided the inspiration for a new attack on the challenge to rid the world of unimaginably destructive nuclear weapons. In his fascinating essay, George describes the resulting effort, which he has led with the same perseverance and dedication that were the trademarks of his success in public office. For me, it has also been a source of great personal pleasure as our close cooperation as colleagues has developed into a close friendship.

EPILOGUE

All these stories are derived from an unusual career. The intermixing of experiences was valuable to me. I can't help but wonder if even the government part of it could be duplicated these days, let alone the movement back and forth from university to government, then business, then back to government, and now back to a life based in the university but mixed with business and government involvement.

I have always considered myself a staunch Republican, and as a young faculty member at MIT I was a lonely supporter of Eisenhower in his successful race against Stevenson. I was proud to serve on the staff of President Eisenhower's Council of Economic Advisers. When the Kennedy administration came to town, I was asked to help think through revisions in the way the U.S. Employment Service operated, and then to work with the Labor Management Committee, composed of top-level business and labor leaders. Later, President Johnson asked me to chair one of his quiet White House task forces, this one on the problem of unemployment in the ghettos. We came up with a good idea and he took it over and ran with it brilliantly, I thought. The effort produced some positive results.

President Nixon asked me to be his secretary of labor, then the first director of the Office of Management and Budget, and then his secretary of the Treasury. This progression of jobs was advantageous for me. I knew the substance of the labor area well and I was quite familiar with the department. With that substance firmly in hand, I could learn about two things I had no experience with: Congress and the press. My teachers were two real pros: Bryce Harlow on the congressional side, and Joe Loftus, who had been the leading labor reporter for the *New York Times*. At the Office of Management and Budget I learned about the whole government, and at the Treasury I had extensive contacts with finance ministers and central bankers all over the world.

I worked for President Reagan in the primaries, in the general election campaigns, and then, after the election, as chairman of the President's Economic Policy Advisory Board. I then became his secretary of state, a position I held for six and a half years.

The tectonic plates of the world shifted during this period. As I worked on all the issues involved, I consulted heavily with members of Congress, both in formal hearings and informal discussions. I had the good fortune of having Senator Richard Lugar, a genuinely constructive man, as head of the Senate Committee on Foreign Relations. Just before I left office, the Senate gave me a farewell luncheon. The event was organized by Senators Lugar and Kennedy, and chaired by Senators Mitchell and Dole. Many senators attended and I thanked them for all their good advice and support. They, in turn, thanked me for all the consultations and presented me with a special award that I value greatly.

Can anyone who has a mixed-up career, moving among university, business, and government posts, get nominated and confirmed to high office today? I hope so. As I work with many others on our effort to find our way toward a world free of nuclear weapons, I am in the good company of most former secretaries of state, secretaries of defense, and national security advisors, with both parties heavily represented. When people praise the bipartisan nature of our effort, we reply that, while it is obvious that both parties are involved, none of us thinks of it as being bipartisan. Our work is *non*partisan. In Congress today, we should be able to carve out at least a few problems that can be addressed on a basis that is free of partisan content.

Two famous Secretaries of the Treasury.

George Shultz presenting Mikhail Gorbachev with an original 1921 Soviet literacy poster
("Long live the sun, May the darkness be hidden."—Aleksandr Pushkin, 1825), June 4, 1990.

As an example of the acrimonious atmosphere in government today, it seems to be extremely difficult, let alone demeaning, to go through the confirmation process. People get discouraged by it and decide not to serve in government. Others have their confirmations delayed for long periods of time, sometimes on the whim of an individual senator who holds up a nomination for some completely unrelated reason. The confirmation process can return, and *must* return, to a commonsense procedure based on sensible questions and on the assumption that honorable people want to do their best to serve honorably as public servants.

There are some encouraging signs. Increasing numbers of voters classify themselves as independent, demonstrating discontent with the extreme partisanship all too frequently on display. In California, voters recently approved an initiative that will reassign the task of drawing the lines of electoral districts away from the hands of politicians and into hands independent of politics. History suggests that civility and sensible legislation are more likely in periods when neither party is in a dominant position. My hopes are high that the current counterproductive acrimony will pass. After all, I had a long career in government and I know that cooperation is possible. With a few ups and downs, I worked in a constructive atmosphere with people who were able, honorable, and dedicated to the best interests of the country.

/ / /

By this time, I hope you are convinced that ideas are of critical importance. Ideas are the catalysts for action; provided with the compass of our principles, they can result in momentous consequences. Combining ideas and action, we can build and achieve a world with even greater safety, productivity, and freedom.

George Shultz demonstrating his farewell gift from NATO foreign ministers, a suitcase containing a miniature train, each car of which represents a NATO country. December 14, 1988.

Looking Back on Reykjavik

On March 24, 2009, George Shultz and Mikhail Gorbachev met in New York City to look back on the U.S.-Soviet exchanges of the late 1980s. The conversation was recorded for use in the three-part television series on George Shultz's life, *Turmoil & Triumph*. Below is a transcript of a portion of that exchange.

> **GEORGE SHULTZ /** Mister President, I remember the first time I met you in Moscow at the time of the Chernenko funeral and our delegation was one of the last you met with. You had been through a long, long, day. So we thought, he's got to be tired. We came there and you were, I said, "fresh as a daisy," and we sat for an hour and a half. I remember you had a whole stack of cards, you shuffled them around, and you never looked at them, and we covered a big range of issues.
>
> Afterwards, we got back to our embassy and I said to then Vice President Bush and all of our delegates, "This is a different man. This is an agile mind. This is a man with a breadth of interest. He's going to be a formidable person to deal with but you can have a conversation with this man. He's terrific."

MIKHAIL GORBACHEV / Indeed that very first meeting was of great importance. What happened was that in the second term President Reagan changed much of his team and a lot changed, not only in your foreign policy, but generally in the policy of the administration. People saw that. We understood that, and I was very sympathetic to that and I think there was a kind of feeling from a distance. Then you and I met many times when we were in office, and after that we continued to cooperate and I am grateful to you for that. You were a very effective leader. And I believe that the fact that there was George Shultz near Ronald Reagan and Shevardnadze near Mikhail Gorbachev was of great importance.

Both foreign ministers were active, were intelligent, had life experience, and experience in politics. And then there was the meeting, the summit at Geneva, which was an amazing event. What happened was that after our first one-on-one with President Reagan we spent about an hour together and then we went to our delegations and my people asked me, "What's your impression?" Generally, the impression of Reagan in our country was bad, but one was cautious about such evaluations. There had been meetings between our leaders for six years and it's hard in such situations to make judgments, including those about President Reagan.

But basically, he was regarded in the Soviet Union as a hawk. Nevertheless, after our first conversation when I talked to my delegation and they asked me what my impression was, I said, "Well, he's a real dinosaur." And later we learned that the same question was put to President Reagan and he said, "Gorbachev is a die-hard Bolshevik." So that was the beginning of our interaction.

GEORGE SHULTZ / I had the opportunity to go to the Soviet Union in the 1970s when I was secretary of the Treasury and I could see that the system had a lot of very intelligent people at the top. I dealt with Kosygin: smart, able to work things out. But the system was not working. I could see that. So when I met you and I saw how able and thoughtful you were, it seemed to me that changes would take place. There were lots of arguments in the United States and people who said, "Nothing can ever change." And I said, "I don't think so. I think things can change. You wait and see." So obviously I didn't know what you were going to do but I was not surprised to see important changes taking place. Perestroika, glasnost—those were big things.

PRESIDENT GORBACHEV / And once again I have to thank you for your understanding because, indeed, our situation was extremely difficult, very challenging. And given that this was the Soviet Union, with its history, given the fact that we were living still in a Stalinist system with minor changes, a system that was not efficient, a system that worked under certain emergency circumstances but when it was necessary to give incentives to stimulate a new initiative, that system was not working. You, I think, were right to notice that.

And it turned out that the nomenklatura, the body and the state bureaucracy, were not ready. Most of them didn't want the change. But there was a sudden nucleus in the Communist Party and in the top leadership, a group of people who understood the change. The people were demanding change. I would say that the productivity in our country was less than one-third of what it was in your country at that time. The productivity in our agriculture was one-fifth that of the United States. We used twice as many metals, cement, and everything else for every unit of production. It was an economy of costs. Everything cost that much more. No system can withstand such pressure. Of course we had the resources. We also saw that there was a scientific and technological revolution and we were not living up to its demands.

GEORGE SHULTZ / Well, one of the things we talked about was the information age. I remember once during a meeting in the Kremlin we had a little side conversation and we talked about it. I said, "We come together and we argue about things all the time. But here is something big, really big, that's going to affect the whole world. It's going to affect you. It's going to affect us. We don't talk about that." We started to talk about it, and it helped move things along.

We sat in the backyard of my house at Stanford and I remember saying to you, "When you and I entered office, the Cold War was as cold as it could get, and when we left office it was all over but the shouting." I said, "What do you think was the turning point?" And you said, without a minute's hesitation, "Reykjavik." I asked, "Why do you say Reykjavik?" You said, "Because there the leaders sat and talked to each other about everything for an extended period, and it was certainly civil." But the results were tremendous.

MIKHAIL GORBACHEV / I still am of the same view. I believe that was the turning point. What happened at Reykjavik was an evolutionary process that led to the elimination of INF missiles. We prepared the ground at Reykjavik. And then, of course, a lot was done also on strategic missiles. Ninety-five percent of the agreement was prepared while you were in office.

When President Reagan and I finished our one-on-one conversation, the initial conversation, I said, "Let us now start discussing the proposals that I brought to Reykjavik. Let us invite Secretary Shultz and Mister Shevardnadze." And I remember you were sitting right in front of me and I started to present my proposals to the president. The president wanted to interfere, to interrupt, and you put your hand on his hand and you said, "Hold on," and we started a very businesslike, very good conversation, on the substance. In two days we covered more ground than sometimes is covered in twenty years.

GEORGE SHULTZ / I think the art of listening is one of the great arts in the world that's underappreciated. And if your ears are always closed and your mouth is open, you don't learn very much. So if you could be quiet and listen to the other guy and try to figure out what's bothering him—what's the essence of his problem—then you can start to solve problems. I always appreciated it because you listened to me and I listened to you, and it helped.

PRESIDENT GORBACHEV / You must listen. Absolutely.

3 DVD SET

TURMOIL & TRIUMPH

THE GEORGE SHULTZ YEARS

The dramatic story of an American Secretary of State and the end of the Cold War.

Free To
CHOOSE
MEDIA

Turmoil & Triumph Documentary Excerpt

George Shultz's career is documented in a three-part public television series entitled *Turmoil & Triumph*. The series pays particular attention to his service as secretary of state during the Reagan years.

The excerpt below is from that television series. It covers the transformative Reagan/Gorbachev summit meeting at Reykjavik, Iceland, on October 11-12, 1986.

NARRATOR / The meeting takes place in a modest building known as Hofdi House. There are no red carpets, no banquets here. Just two men and their foreign ministers, meeting in this unpretentious seaside house to decide the fate of the world.

The two sides enter the house and move to their places around a table in a small room. If Shultz and Reagan expected only a preparatory meeting with a casual agenda, Mikhail Gorbachev quickly surprises them.

REEVES / When Reagan walked in that room, the first sign of what was going to happen was, in comes Gorbachev lugging this briefcase full of papers which he proceeds to unload onto the table.

NARRATOR / As the meeting begins, Gorbachev proceeds to present a stunning array of arms concessions.

MIKHAIL GORBACHEV / I proposed that the entire triad of strategic nuclear weapons, sea-based, land-based missiles, and aircraft, be counterbalanced on both sides by cutting every element in half. This was a very important proposal on our part.

Richard Reeves
Historian - Univ. of Southern California

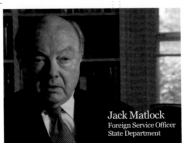

Jack Matlock
Foreign Service Officer
State Department

NARRATOR / Gorbachev also agrees to extend the Anti-Ballistic Missile Treaty for another ten years. But there is a catch. The U.S. will have to limit its testing of the Strategic Defense Initiative (SDI) to the laboratory. In spite of this restriction, it is an impressive number of Soviet concessions.

Foreign Service Officer Jack Matlock was a note-taker in the meeting.

JACK MATLOCK / Gorbachev definitely wanted to give Reagan a proposal he considered so forthright, and meeting so many American goals, that it would permit him to persuade Reagan to drop his devotion to strategic defense.

NARRATOR / As the two sides break for lunch, the Americans are impressed.

JOURNALIST VO / "Mr. President, have you made any real progress?"

REAGAN ON TV / "We're not through."

JOURNALIST VO / "Are you going to meet again, sir?"

REAGAN ON TV / "Yes."

NARRATOR / Shultz is so pleased with the morning's progress he says, "They're coming our way." Disarmament expert Paul Nitze calls the Soviet proposals "the best they have ever made."

In the afternoon, the talks continue. Gorbachev rarely asks his foreign minister, Eduard Shevardnadze, to join the discussion. Reagan, on the other hand, frequently relies on his secretary of state to present the Americans' bargaining position.

MATLOCK / But Reagan and Shultz had a different kind of relationship, and Reagan knew that Shultz knew the details of these things better than he did, and could explain them better.

GORBACHEV / I've always said that Secretary of State Shultz was a major figure when we began to move forward in addressing problems and began talking about the future.

NARRATOR / The short Icelandic day comes to an end. Reagan suggests letting the diplomatic staffs take over the task of working out the wording of an agreement to be discussed the next day.

Overnight, the negotiating teams work feverishly to hammer out the details of a new disarmament treaty. In the confined space of Hofdi House, memos are written, calls are made to respective capitals, copies and translations made, changes approved, and revisions negotiated.

But as a new day begins and the meeting resumes, one fact becomes very clear. Mikhail Gorbachev is firm. He demands no testing of SDI anywhere but in the laboratory.

SHULTZ / Gorbachev kept hammering on the strategic defense and he said to President Reagan, "Mister President, why do you need a defense against ballistic missiles if we're agreeing to abolish them?"

GORBACHEV / We were not requiring something outrageous. We said we don't want that research to be in space. But if the United States were allowed to do research in laboratories and we cut our weapons, why start an arms race in outer space?

NARRATOR / In Gorbachev's mind, the equation is simple. Test SDI only in laboratories. Further negotiations attempt to eliminate any need for a shield in space to stop ballistic missiles.

GORBACHEV VO / "You can conduct laboratory research in SDI. After the ten years, we can completely eliminate all nuclear weapons."

REAGAN VO / "If we both eliminate nuclear weapons, why would there be a concern if one side wants to build defensive systems just in case?"

GORBACHEV VO / "Mr. President, we are close to a mutually acceptable formula. Don't think we have evil designs! We don't!"

NARRATOR / Reagan may not have been sure of evil designs, but he knew his precious Star Wars Initiative was a chess piece Gorbachev wanted off the table. Reagan is unwilling to limit research on a program, even though its feasibility is far from proven.

REEVES / I don't know whether he ever thought it would work. I don't think anybody else thought that it would work. But I do know that he thought, and he was very quick to pick up on the fact, that Gorbachev was terrified by the thought of SDI. And why was Gorbachev terrified? Not because he was that afraid of the Americans, but because he had no economy to match a buildup of a new weapons system.

NARRATOR / The two sides are closer than they have ever been to the elimination of a whole class of nuclear missiles. As the pressure mounts in the room, Reagan finally blurts out:

REAGAN VO / "It would be fine with me if we eliminated all nuclear weapons!"

NARRATOR / Without hesitation, Gorbachev shoots back with words that will live forever in the history of summit meetings:

GORBACHEV VO / "We can do that! Let's eliminate them all. All nuclear weapons! Bombers, everything else. We can eliminate them!"

Condoleezza Rice

NARRATOR / Since the end of World War II, the world has dreamed of somehow getting the awful genie of nuclear Armageddon back in the bottle. Now here, in a small house on the Icelandic sea, the superpower leaders are at last speaking of ridding their relationship of nuclear weapons. What has been an impossible dream now rests on one word: laboratory.

HENRY KISSINGER / It was a strange negotiation because nobody had expected that they would reach that point. I certainly was amazed that offer was made.

RICE / I can certainly identify with what they faced at Reykjavik when George Shultz and Ronald Reagan heard the words, "Yes, we can do this, but you're going to have to stop testing in space."

MATLOCK / I think it was a mistake on Gorbachev's part not to discuss it in greater detail and not to explain just directly. "Ron, you've got to understand. My people see this as an offensive strategy."

NARRATOR / Ronald Reagan is eager to say yes to the negotiated agreements.

SHULTZ / And so was I for that matter. And so we had all of these dramatic agreements, and the Soviets made them all conditional on confining the research on the Strategic Defense Initiative to the laboratory, which we interpreted as: they wanted to kill it.

NARRATOR / As the allotted meeting time ticks off, the two leaders are aware of what is at stake. They plead with each other.

REAGAN VO / "We should not stop because of one word. I'm asking you to change your mind as a favor to me. So hopefully we can go out and bring peace to the world. "

GORBACHEV VO / "I can't do it! But if we could agree to ban research in space, I'd sign in two minutes! It's laboratory or nothing!"

NARRATOR / Reagan scribbles a note to Shultz asking, "Am I wrong?"

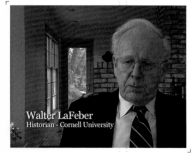

Walter LaFeber
Historian - Cornell University

Shultz at last realizes Reagan is determined to keep space testing. There will be no giving up the sleeves from the vest. He whispers back:

"No, you are right."

WALTER LAFEBER / Shultz at several points was willing to compromise SDI in order to get other things. But once Reagan took the position that SDI was not negotiable—that it could not stay simply in the laboratory but it had to be tested outside the laboratory—Shultz went right down the line with Reagan. Shultz knew that this was not the sort of Reagan of caricatures—that Reagan had thought about these issues and that he was deeply committed to SDI. Shultz was not going to resign over an issue like that, even if some kind of agreement with the Soviet Union was as close as it was at Reykjavik.

NARRATOR / It has all come down to one word and Reagan, at last, will not agree to it. The president says, "Come on, George." Reagan and his secretary of state get to their feet and the Reykjavik Summit is over. They have come so close to accomplishing a diplomatic miracle.

MATLOCK / It was a glum mood as we left the Hofdi House in Reykjavik, faces absolutely as if they had lost their closest relative. And you know the pictures of it show it. Look at the pictures of the two coming out of that, and you know that it is not good news.

NARRATOR / As Reagan reaches his car, Gorbachev asks once more:

GORBACHEV VO / "There is still time Mr. President. We could go back inside to the bargaining table. I don't know what more I could have done."

REAGAN VO / "You could have said yes."

SHULTZ / And I rode with the president in the car back to the embassy where he was staying, and somebody asked me why I looked tired and disappointed. And I said because I was tired and disappointed.

NARRATOR / Shultz's disturbing appearance at the press conference following the last meeting further convinces some that the summit has been a failure.

SHULTZ ON TV / "So in the end, we are deeply disappointed at this outcome."

SHULTZ / But if I had thought about it a little more, I'd have taken a deep breath and said, we didn't... weren't... able to make closure but we made a huge amount of progress, which we did. Gigantic.

REEVES / Everybody came away with conflicting views of what had happened. But in the end, what had happened was Reagan and Gorbachev had stripped each other down to the essentials, and from then on Reagan and Gorbachev trusted each other.

DON OBERDORFER / Reykjavik was something that will go down in history as a very important milestone when the two leading countries of the nuclear world began to deal with it, and deal with it directly.

LAFEBER / I think what Reykjavik proved to Gorbachev was that Reagan was not going to change his position on SDI. And I think at that point, Gorbachev had to push SDI aside in order to get what he really, really wanted and needed very badly in the Soviet Union, which was a series of arms controls to reduce the Soviet budget. I'm not sure how much Reagan realized this, but I'm sure Shultz did.

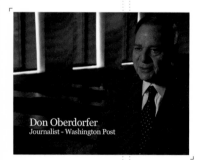

Don Oberdorfer
Journalist - Washington Post

NARRATOR / For all its appearance of failure, Reykjavik has actually been a success. The leaders have made enormous progress at controlling nuclear weapons and have spoken with an openness and frankness as never before.

Years later, in the 1990s, George Shultz will ask Mikhail Gorbachev exactly when he thought the Cold War ended. The Soviet leader will answer in one word:

"Reykjavik!"

Biography

One of George Shultz's favorite days…when he piloted an F-15.

GEORGE PRATT SHULTZ / George Pratt Shultz has had a distinguished career in government, in academia, and in the world of business. He is one of a handful of individuals who have held four different federal cabinet posts; he has taught at three of this country's greatest universities; and for eight years he was president of a major engineering and construction company.

Mr. Shultz was born in New York City on December 13, 1920, and grew up in Englewood, New Jersey. He attended Princeton University, graduating in 1942 with a B.A. in economics. Shortly after graduation, he enlisted in the Marine Corps and served through 1945. He then resumed his studies, this time at MIT, where he earned a Ph.D. in industrial economics in 1949. From 1948 to 1957 he taught at MIT, taking a leave of absence in 1955 to serve as a senior staff economist on President Eisenhower's Council of Economic Advisors.

In 1957, Mr. Shultz joined the faculty of the University of Chicago Graduate School of Business as a professor of industrial relations. He was named dean five years later. From 1968 to 1969 he was a fellow at the Center for Advanced Study in the Behavioral Sciences at Stanford University.

He returned to government when he was appointed secretary of labor by President Nixon in 1969. In June 1970, he became director of the Office of Management and Budget. In May 1972, he was named secretary of the Treasury, a post he held for two years. During this period, Mr. Shultz also served as chairman of the Council on Economic Policy, negotiated a series of trade protocols with the Soviet Union, and represented the United States at the Tokyo meeting on the General Agreement of Tariffs and Trade.

Mr. Shultz left government service in 1974 to become president and director of the Bechtel Group, Inc., where he remained until 1982. While at Bechtel, he maintained his close ties with the academic world by joining the faculty of Stanford University.

Mr. Shultz held two key positions in the Reagan administration: chairman of the President's Economic Policy Advisory Board (1981-82) and secretary of state (1982-89). As secretary of state, he played a key role in implementing a foreign policy that led to the successful conclusion of the Cold War and the development of strong relationships between the United States and the countries of the Asia-Pacific region including China, Japan, and the ASEAN countries.

After leaving office, Mr. Shultz rejoined the Bechtel Group as director and senior counselor. He also rejoined Stanford as professor of international economics at the Graduate School of Business and as distinguished fellow at the Hoover Institution. In 2001, Mr. Shultz was named the Thomas W. and Susan B. Ford Distinguished Fellow at the Hoover Institution.

In January 1989, Mr. Shultz was awarded the Medal of Freedom, the nation's highest civilian honor. He is also a recipient of the Seoul Peace Prize (1992), the West Point Sylvanus Thayer Award (1992), the Eisenhower Medal for Leadership and Service (2001), the Reagan Distinguished American Award (2002), and the Association for Diplomatic Studies and Training's Ralph Bunche Award for Diplomatic Excellence (2002). Other honors awarded in 2002 include the Elliot Richardson Prize for Excellence and Integrity in Public Service, the James H. Doolittle Award, and the John Witherspoon Medal for Distinguished Statesmanship. The George Shultz National Foreign Affairs Training Center in Arlington, Virginia, was dedicated in a ceremony on May 29, 2002.

Mr. Shultz was named a distinguished fellow of the American Economic Association in 2005. He received the American Spirit Award from the National World War II Museum in 2006. In 2007, he received the George Marshall Award from the United States Agency for International Development and the Truman Medal for Economic Policy. He received the Rumford Prize from the American Academy of Arts & Sciences in 2008 and the Commandant's Leadership Award from the Marine Corps-Law Enforcement Foundation in 2009.

Mr. Shultz's publications include *Putting Our House in Order: A Citizen's Guide to Social Security and Health Care Reform*, with John B. Shoven (2008), *Turmoil and Triumph: My Years as Secretary of State* (1993), *Economic Policy Beyond the Headlines* (1977), *Workers and Wages in the Urban Labor Market* (1970), *Guidelines, Informal Controls, and the Marketplace* (1966), *Strategies for the Displaced Worker: Confronting Economic Change* (1966), *Management Organization and the Computer* (1960), *Labor Problems: Cases and Readings* (1953), *The Dynamics of a Labor Market* (1951), and *Pressures on Wage Decisions* (1950).

Mr. Shultz holds honorary degrees from Notre Dame, Columbia, Loyola, Pennsylvania, Rochester, Princeton, Carnegie-Mellon, CUNY, Yeshiva University, the Weizmann Institute of Science, Baruch College of New York, the Hebrew University of Jerusalem, Tbilisi State University in the Republic of Georgia, Technion, Keio University in Tokyo, Williams College, and Peking University.

Mr. Shultz is chairman of the Governor of California's Economic Advisory Board, the Advisory Council chair of the Precourt Institute for Energy Efficiency at Stanford University, and chair of the MIT Energy Initiative External Advisory Board. He serves on the boards of directors of Accretive Health and Fremont Group.

But George
I have to talk to you
the Russians are calling!!

Secretary Shultz and Israeli Prime Minister Yitzhak Shamir immediately after the P.M.'s aide suddenly walked out wearing an outrageous wig.

Picture Credits

Bechtel Corporation: cover, jacket flap, 16 (top), 18, 34 (top), 34 (bottom)

Ronald Reagan Presidential Foundation: 14

White House : 15, 16 (middle), 21 (top), 21 (bottom), 22, 24, 28, 45, 52, 57 (top),
57 (bottom), 58, 62/63, 64, 69 (top), 76, 80/81, 86 (bottom), 109,
117 (top), 117 (bottom), 118 (bottom), 120/121, 148/149

University of Chicago: 16 (bottom), 31, 32/33, 114

George Shultz: 23 (top), 105, 142

AFL-CIO: 36

Matty Stern/USIA: 42, 150/151

Beit Hatfutsot, Photo Archive, Tel Aviv: 46

L. Bianco, Geneva: 67

Cynthia Johnson/Time & Life Images/Getty Images: 75, 90 (top)

William Eaton/Los Angeles Times: 83-Los Angeles Times, © 1981.
Reprinted with permission.

White House/Getty Images News: 90 (bottom)

Dirck Halstead/Getty Images News: 96

Paul Conrad: 102-Paul Conrad © 1988. Reprinted with permission.

Ronald Reagan Presidential Library/Archive Photos/Getty Images: 106 (top)

Kevin Winter/Getty Images Entertainment: 106 (bottom)

Saul Loeb/AFP/Getty Images: 110

Free To Choose Network: 122, 129, 130, 132, 133, 134, 135, 136, 137, 138, 139, 140,
141

U.S. Air Force: 144